empire

Camino del Sol

A Latina and Latino Literary Series

empire

poems by

Xochiquetzal Candelaria

THE UNIVERSITY OF ARIZONA PRESS • TUCSON

The University of Arizona Press

© 2011 Xochiquetzal Candelaria

www.uapress.arizona.edu

Library of Congress Cataloging-in-Publication Data
appear on the last printed page of this book.

Publication of this book is made possible in part by the proceeds of a permanent
endowment created with the assistance of a Challenge Grant from the National
Endowment for the Humanities, a federal agency.

Manufactured in the United States of America on acid-free, archival-quality paper
containing a minimum of 30% post-consumer waste and processed chlorine free.

16   15   14   13   12   11   6   5   4   3   2   1

For my parents, Luis and Lupe Candelaria,

and

In Memory of June Jordan (1936–2002)

The others are unreachable not because they are impenetrable, but because they are infinite.

—**Octavio Paz,** *An Erotic Beyond: Sade*

contents

I

II

III

I

Mexico, 1910

A bullet comes later for Dolores,

after the war,

a shock of pain in her chest

as if thrown

from her horse,

a brown stallion I imagine,

grazing on a solitary hill

above Torreón.

On a night so clear

you can make out

the long muscles of his neck

as he chews,

his chewing marking time

for the city of embers

Dolores stokes

while the other women sleep.

Two sisters, side by side

during the day,

one holding a cartridge belt,

the other firing,

are lying curled back to back.

Maybe Dolores thinks

they look like butterfly wings

as she topples a steeple of ash.

I call her Dolores

after Our Lady of Many Sorrows,

not because of the Mauser at her side

or the many times she will use it

but because, as a child, she falls

in love with a goat

she calls *Mother,*

and the other children laugh,

and still she feels something about

the hoofed animal

is sacred.

Its look as old as hunger

as it gnaws on a strip of hide

tied to a post, so bare

even the flies won't land,

while Dolores at the well works

hand over hand,

and the water stains her

skirt a darker red.

If I said she suddenly stopped working,

hearing the goat

clop away, leather

band in its mouth,

I'd be lying.

If I said she didn't follow

it out of town,

I'd be lying too.

I think she grew to leave

little by little—

first a call, then a calling

to ride past the whitewashed wall

broken in places,

leaking dirt into dirt.

Migration

The white blue of daylight shrinks to a rip,

and the geese seem to slip through

but don't. They crush on through the stitched

darkness, past the New Mexican/Mexican *migration*

border, year after year. It is the movement

I want to remember, illiterate and surviving

like my great-grandmother mending

the pants of soldiers bunking down in the scrub grass,

her needles made of cactus spine embedded

in a sack of goods strapped to her back.

sence of survival!

One peso for washing, two for sewing.

The unwritten story goes: she sold more

than salvaged clothes, marching with a traveling

brothel. I don't think words can explain it,

the indiscriminate passing and desire to persist.

I've seen one picture of her in front

of a clapboard church in Earlimart, California,

hands together, plump face belying

the white feathers barely visible under a veil.

If I can say anything, I'll say I descended

from a migrant bird. Even in the fading picture,

freedom

she seems to be telling whoever held

the camera to hurry up by standing perfectly still.

Primavera

Gold and silver tinsel skirts hid diesel tires

of flatbed trucks as they rumbled down Main Street.

The ones festooned with thousands of crepe flowers,

charioted girls in taffeta dresses perched

on wicker chairs, waving as if to say good-bye

and hello equally and to everyone—to the widow

Mrs. Larson, who wore a light-blue Sunday suit

and kept the front room of her house a gallery

for her late husband's photography; to Pedro,

who swept the streets and scraped gum

from sidewalks most days; to Willy and his five

cousins on holiday from Vacaville. These town

beauties, who ate beef stroganoff and *pan dulce*

like the rest of us, who might have split their lips

in recent history on the saddle of the 25 cent

yellow mechanical horse outside Louie's store,

were on their way. Not to a place, of course. We all

knew that; they were just on their way to us

and for us to smile at as we ate caramel corn and hotdogs.

Cortés and Cannon

Before Cortés lops off a messenger's

hands and has another trampled,

before the branding and burning,

there is wonderment

and, for a moment, endearment

as Cortés dances, off beat, around

the long neck of his field piece.

Stroking it, he whispers into its mouth,

then cocks his ear to the darkness.

He does this several times, then orders

his men to lie on the ground in homage to the iron.

Clapping his cracked hands,

he speaks in a tongue of corkscrew

and wing, telling the Totonacs to bring

themselves closer. And like well-meaning

friends, bearing glinting quetzal feathers

and silver cactus milk, they laugh,

pretending to understand,

believing him wild with love

for the enormous, hollow thing

he has hauled from the hull of his ship.

Many Years After

German Shepherds,   their muzzles wedged

between fence posts,   growling,   water pools in the empty   sound

of spruce trees, funneling   the light.

Hours ago, a family: two towheaded boys scrambled   ahead.

"You're not   far now,"   the father said,

his leg

gashed   above the knee,   his wife

wheezing.

Dead   leaves sound like   panting beneath

my feet.

Without entering a door,   I arrive   inside,

the right nave completely gone,   bleached planks   disappearing into dirt.

My body casts its   shadow   beneath a painting of shadows

barely visible   on a wall   scoured by a blast.

Did it begin   one night as a whistle   only dogs   hear?

A branch scrapes floorboards

in a wet staccato,   graffiti reading: *COME CLOSER!*

I want to scrawl: *In Memory of Flight*

until, standing on a bench,   I see bits of pigment

                  holding together   the convert's

eyes,   the curves of   four dogs crouching.   It is almost

dark now.   The mouth   of Saint Jude   is a

blue   scar.

Empire #1

Five and Dime Store, 1949

With the patience of a teacher,

my five-year-old mother repeats the word

for the perspiring salesclerk,

her small brown hand reaching

over the counter to mime the size

of the little black pincer

as if he might not

yet know the word

but would recognize it by shape.

How to explain the little black embrace

you lace through a twirl of freshly washed

hair. In Spanish they are called *horquillas*

but in English "va-ee-peens."

What will it take to make the salesclerk

understand; this is a matter of beauty.

A Daughter

Sergio mentioned the hills,

how he spotted my dad and me

on the back roads. What I remember

is how we stood stunned from the heat

of the run, the view of the valley:

fifteen sheep grazing near

a cypress tree tucked in the hip

of the closest hill, my father's eyes

watching the sand rise off a path.

But perhaps I was hampered by the view,

and Sergio knew something was missing.

Perhaps my dad stood dreaming

of something he wished he had

done, that would have been his own,

the way he weighed in each hand

a granite and shale stone. Maybe I

just needed to see my father looking out

on the land, at the groomed plots

framed with boulders and thistle,

because this way he appeared wise

to me, knew the size of a healthy heifer,

the sickly shoots of adolescent wheat.

There on the edge of an overhang

instead of down in the city below,

I would have nodded *yes* to Sergio,

agreed my dad picked up the rocks

to protect me. I would have let the boy

giggle, as if he had stumbled upon the secret.

Parade

In Quintana Roo, a town bereft of its name

after the last man and woman ate a final

tortilla and tucked themselves in the river, before

the soldiers of this poem slid razorback

to the outdoor oven, cleaning their heels on mats

of yak fur, waiting for the crisis to begin,

there were days and days that didn't much matter;

no one died or was born, no one touched lit

matches to firecracker fuses, no courtship

paint–smeared faces or feather headdress sun

salutations, no send-offs or ritual washings

with deer soap and sage; just days and days

of sewing, cooking, singing, then sitting

by a window, not even wondering what others

in some far-off place might be doing, just days

and days of heat, light, wind, heat, light, wind.

1973

A buzzing swells, breaks,

      returns in the form of mechanical moans

before becoming a young man's shredded voice

reciting word problems, his beard barely able to disguise

his boyish cheeks. *If they take the city   if they storm the palace*

how will we explain it?

Tapping the side of the loudspeaker

to introduce time and   the girl to his left,   who looks down

at her coffee-stained notebook   as if to spell us there.

X-o-c-h-i-q-u-e-t-z-a-l.

        I was given

an Aztec goddess–

flower-bird name

as the last planes   released their official Agent

Orange on leaves   leading out of the Mekong,

my father sticking

     my feet in his mouth to warm them.

Light feeding   across the sky   as if caught by an arrow of

geese . . .

                 ☙

At seven, I'm called the Bird Lady.

Hostages are returning,   my uncle

still alive

in the New Mexican desert.

I hear two volumes: *loud and louder.*

My mother's newspaper

clippings curling in the deep drawer of the living room

end table.

My father lifting

       his wrist

             to read the Golden Nugget

digital watch

for the 40th time.

He discovered it in the gutter near

       our front porch.   My sister and I, fighting

            our laughter,   fail

to understand   lost things.

The beginning of the end

must have   its own exit,

own rhythm.

M-i-s-s/i-s-s/i-p-p-i,   I repeat,

      while practicing to dance

            the Four Corners, the Smurf,

while looking up

       at Tiny Baby

           Tender Love,

her underpants gone,

revealing

the little hole she peed from.

Seven sounds like a boy's age,

                so I call myself Frankie,

call myself on the rotary phone by dialing our number

to announce the good news.

                    It's a new decade; I've shed the last cell of the

beginning

of the coup d'état.   I'm a year closer

        to the presidency, I think

in the hot-lunch line   of San Juan Bautista Elementary

the year my aunt returns

        (from Paris? Madrid? where she danced

as a skeleton)

to live in our back room;

the day I vote

        for Jimmy Carter in Ms. Moreno's class,

letting Javier look up my skirt   because he doesn't speak

English.

Vanishing!   a word I'll repeat all afternoon

to mimic Spanish,

        infinity, and my mother

wearing only water,

a wetness that signals

I'm not alive to write this.

At the end of the Second World War,   her limbs shiver,

                                                                        bob all afternoon

in a water-filled wine barrel,

rescuing her tiny brown body from the San Joaquín sun.

A lucky one,

or maybe it was another

                        whose name   escapes me now,

lost in a blizzard,

the one

                        I tried to stare   through,

                                        wondering if I could

write something   I believed in.

Caught in the Eye of the Sun

I watch the cobblestones climb each other

as I walk, head down in the heat, repeating:

say it isn't María, my sister.

Say it's the other, my grandmother,

whom my father, a country away,

is calling about. I want to say, here

in Guanajuato, the silver city

known for its mummies,

the soul of Cervantes has taken

my grandmother with him.

Taken her yellow eyes and spindly hair

and left a painted sugar skull in honor of her smile.

By the time I reach the phone booth,

my prayer will begin to be answered.

I'll have bargained like the boy in the *zócalo*

selling mangos and plastic jewelry,

holding in each hand a fist of trinkets,

the ones he wants me to take raised higher.

Empire #2

Poet

I wonder what he recited: metal on metal, glass

shattering, circuits blowing, the hiss of grease,

coolant geyser? If my brother's lip split like a cherry

or gave like cloth as his head hit the controls, if he recited

fruit and blood at the same time, feared the oncoming

lights as much as the interrogator's invectives. If

momentarily he felt seconds tingle, hands reading

feathers, his chest a library, night air

scrawled with citrus as they lifted him not gently onto

the page. If he imagined we knew nothing

as we looked up at the stars, dreaming ourselves among them.

Although You Can Take It—

nothing about the picture

suggests it belonged

to anyone, the tincture

of a polite puddle has long

been blind, and Orpheus perpetually

hides his vivid purse,

a Coke in hand. Casually,

he sings a verse

to León plums. Even the circus

of unclean fruit is out of focus—

a blushing trampoline below.

True, it's just a snapshot

pilfered from a dumpster/feedlot

for mice. And Orpheus,

a vendor who doesn't own the dust

on his pears. Welcome to San Juan,

Sir. Pay in quetzals if you can.

A Question

The woman in the building across from me

hauls onto the fire escape a yucca plant

and squeezes it between a crate

of herbs and a sapling fern tree.

She looks a lot like me from twenty feet away.

A forelock lies sweaty against her cheek

as if she's forgotten to fix herself.

I put my thumbs and forefingers

to my eye and frame her. I am reminded

of those Chinese boxes made of red paper,

inside one is another holding another,

until at the center sits the tiniest mockery

and celebration of the cell itself.

She looks haggard but happy here, five flights

up, bending over a fat leaf as if admiring herself

in the waxy surface. Then she opens up

the jewel-case of her voice,

and I remember how once my sister asked

my mother which one of us sang better.

My mother paused from sewing as if adding

seventeen to seventy-five and said we sounded

the same. Good or bad, who knows.

Each of us now watches the empty,

open mouth of the other.

II

Esta Palabra

How I slip into it like a hot bath,

his name at my feet, then thighs,

circling each breast, how I float

in his name, never lost

in the din of names I know. How

I dress in the scent of his name

at night, the pepper-sweet oil

triggering sweat glands filling

thousands of tiny tubs in the hollows

of my neck, how one

brown syllable grows like debt,

spans weeks, then years

before it breaks

and slides back to blue,

leaving Mojave wind

like a thicket of lions,

wailing at the heat, the line

of sheets, wailing for milk

and keys, my eyes filling

with vowels until finally

I begin forming in my head

a row of wet-calf words,

each one knowing where to press

and where to rest, where to separate

and remain together.

Sappho

Fragments—a line,

sometimes eight,

one scrap found stuffed in the mouth

of a mummified cat.

Let's say we know this

as we know the cat

once roamed

light-footed through a garden

of hyacinth and violets,

inking between the legs of guests,

sheer linen–

dressed dancers, lute players.

Everyone drunk.

In one jump the cat lands on a whitewashed wall

between shards of broken glass

on a cliff giving way to the sea.

Its silver-rimmed eyes

reflect the tincture of moonlight off water,

a lucency

that also falls through the branches of a fig tree

into the room of two women.

The older one

mouths something to herself over the young one's

lit breasts,

something like *let me see this forever,*

before she cries for the simple way the breasts darken

as the shadows shift.

The young lover, who will leave by morning,

turns toward

the wall, offers only her hair,

a dark, tangled nest

the aging woman will remember

and later call, despite the absence of light,

the evening star.

What kind of creature does this?

Reinvents the body despite the body's rejection?

Imagines dust and debris

of love's collapse to be great arms in the bed of the sky?

Who gathers from hair

constellations,

feeding them

to the hungry strays that call through the night air?

The Report

In kanji characters, his name, skeletal
like a ship stripped of sails,

seems to hover in the brined night air
where his wigged head would be

had he been lecturing
on the nature of betrayal,

had we called to him
and he angled to answer

our absurd questions
about fathers. Those

are my baby teeth glued
to the yard of his mizzenmast.

I'm trying to find the commons
and live without meat.

Almost out of frame, he admits
he sold the rigging.

New season: tomorrow,
we lay waste to the fields.

On Language

A blue pail left floating

washes up on the pitted, rocky shore,
wedges between boulders dark as
prehistory, a place the utterance goes it alone.

He says, "That's how strong my love is."

The utterance overlooks the ocean on two sides,
circles the town square,
where kids play cricket in the sand, explores
the ruins of an immigration station and prison
blown up in 1963,

the year he was born.

Switchgrass molding to human shapes.

Sitting in the morning sun,

she says, "Is there a solution in the passageway?"

Eyes and ears making women of all of us?

"In songs to remember,"

she writes a city, and ipso facto

it is and can never be.

He writes a city fading,

and birds begin feeding

on scraps of paper.

Between the House and the Hill

This boy lying face down

in my sleep pushes around jars of jelly,

waking me the night he is found

so I can drag him from the wet ground

and clean his blackened belly,

this boy lying face down

who is somehow bound

to me, this hunted herdsman, refugee

waking me the night he is found.

Am I to dress him in an open gown,

bless the holes in his chest with tea

leaves? This boy lying face down,

permeating even the simplest sound,

with the crack in the door he slowly

cries, waking me the night he is found,

lips parted to my blue-black ground,

whispering red vetch inside me,

this slender boy lying down,

waking me the night he is found.

Boom

I wake up as rabbits; nothing but fur

against fur, a rabbit in ruins, twin spires

of my ears eavesdropping on conversations,

the asymptote of me forever rising, forever

falling, offering myself at

market in exchange for fare.

I burrow below the Treasury Building,

chomping on silver shavings, glowing E

Pluribus Unum at night

(dreaming of my cousin

of haute couture lying

against a woman's back,

my matted sister, skinned brother),

glistening like Dubai silk on

LCD billboards tracking homes,

begotten like rabbits but never built.

Once I became blind

as a bunny who nursed at the teat of my dog, Elsa,

winning fourth prize at the jumbo fair. Clare

claimed everyone had to win something

because of inflation and the new judges.

My blue-ribbon reading: *A Rabbit's*
Rabbit for the Cold Man in the Moon.

The Message

A frog, a bird, a mouse, and five arrows

make Darius turn his horse and retreat to the hills.

The moment the eye becomes the ear.

—Alarm bells sounding as all the little

golden packages fall from the shelves, silt shaking

before tumbling to the paved road below. For instance,

perhaps we need to act and you might never know unless you see:

a radio with a baby-blue Bakelite dial set to six, the Roman

numerals glinting in the dark next to a 16-mm film of your

father furrowing his brow, head cocked to the side as if

he's listening to a *compañero* tell a story about a man siring

a child instead of sailing to Veracruz, the skidding,

thump, wack, blam, milk, feather, sweaty silky blubber, fresh

boots, the opening of an orange parachute snapping as it holds.

Empire #3

Marriage

My brother-in-law walks, unannounced,

through the front door, passes me,

and pulls a beer from the refrigerator.

A new heaviness

about him. A man who didn't mind

my sister was Mexican; a man who tried

to explain to my parents Reagan's

trickle-down-theory as if they

were hard of hearing now sits with me

in the kitchen, takes one of my

cigarettes from the counter, and starts

to weep, his voice breaking in the air

like a hard ball falling down steps.

I didn't expect to share a smoke,

let alone care about him.

I don't say much, mostly I listen

to him mispronounce, over and over,

the name of a man

he could kill, a clear torture tied

in his eyes, a pain so whittled and dark.

Core Greater Than Three Solar Masses

Everything that exists, from the tiniest to this,

is still expanding.

Dark form spreading: music,

surplus, seeds.

This radiation yours,

your mother's, the mother before.

Successive touching

of floating cities.

Do scientists know if we will

contract and meet again

or if we are open forever?

Is a galaxy a family?

A state (with arms reaching

out from a

central bulge)?

The lovers (drifting),

harboring small stars,

not wanting to let particulates go

pulsing under pressure,

beginning to glow.

The Irises

Their green sepals begin like mouths, forming the word

okay, turning over at the tips to say

yes, then *oh yes.*

Three deep-purple petals smoldering give way

to three more giving way.

Fire breaks through as a seam in the center.

These are messengers remembering that to speak

is to bloom and to bloom

is to sing and sing and sing.

Blue Alert

The hand on the handle
turns the lever to three.

The light near the sunlight,
the man by the tree

selling lemons as limes
and limes for the rind.

The light near the sunlight
at a quarter to three

burns by dust from coal
by the sea. Three men

browned and three more
blackened

by the impossible sun
at the heart of attack.

In the back pantry near
coal by the sea, leak lemons

like sewage down to the sea.

Put your hand in my hand,

leading out of the light to the cool

cave, to the milk night.

The Novitiate

Before I lie down,
place the heels of my feet
on the edge of the worn
wooden bed frame;
my sister moves
swiftly to the shelf,
plucks a book. One hand steadies
the heavy, black binding,
her eyes focused on
diagrams of the body.
The beauty mark above her upper lip
rises as she asks me
if I want her to look.
I could schedule
an appointment,
or purchase a predictor kit.
As she turns to shut
the window, I see light
filling tree branches
we played on every summer,
hear a lawnmower
a few houses down,
smell barbeque coals
and lighter fluid
mixing with her perfume.
I lift my skirt
and prop my head
up on pillows. She explains:
"This might feel cool," and slowly
she peers inside.
She says it would
swell a deep purple,
blood blotching
the skin, the skin
showing signs.

Leda Explains

That lean, strong arm without

an arm. That absolutely dart-
away-raw-reeling-sky
rat incrementally
crept up and leered at my

knee: a convenient arrangement
(the night unrolled, his beak
invisible) I brought
down my unflinching cheek.

Christmas, 1964

It is easy enough
when the man you just met
lifts his arms, beckoning
you to turn, and your body
obeys, and the ladies
of the house have made
four trays of chicken *mole,*
laid them out with pozole, tamales,
spiced rum. You will be here awhile,
I suspect, if the Christmas
lights keep chasing your pulse
around the room. You will step
and shake long enough to break
a cool sweat, the net of your
arms trawling the dance floor
for more. Your grandmother
thought you could get pregnant
if you moved this way. Maybe
it's true. Children are swimming
through the room. The one circling
your hips wants to cut in,
rise to the surface of your chest,
and rock. You are practicing
surrender here with your whole
body, so that when the time comes,
you will say *yes,*
when later you will think,
how am I going to do this?

Here We Are

St. Hildegarde of Bingen might have had a word for it

(more red than sleep, deeper than confess),

where the skin silks around the town of your left eye,

this territory so close to sight. I want to put the tip of

my nose, no my lips, no my lower lip, there and breathe.

I'd gladly leave everything behind: the toaster,

chain-link fence, church bells, migration,

full moons, seaweed, mulberry, urgency, feathers, thinking.

After Sex

He takes a pear

and bites off

the dark bruise,

so the white meat

sparkles in the summer sun,

and politely he turns

it for her to bite in a new

place, and they are both

crushing, sucking, and nodding

as if they agree on something.

Chimayo, New Mexico

This is happening in the back room

of the unpainted adobe church adorned

with wooden double doors,

visible behind us in the photograph.

I'm the one in braids, shielding

my eyes, while my sister raises

three fingers. A clear day

the reason we get to play outside,

why there exists another photograph

of my sister with a sprig of rosemary

in her mouth, gazing up as I climb

Mary to deliver a crown of poppies.

Later, I take a picture of a terra-cotta tile,

one edge imprinted with a dog's paw,

a primitive photograph itself.

Contemplating a shot of our father

while he rests his hands on a polished pew,

I turn instead toward a painting where Mary

Magdalene kneels in a red dress,

hair dripping, Jesus's hand close enough to feel

heat from her lips. Two strips of purple fabric

cloak the painting like a veil,

as if their bodies formed a face, but none of this

will be visible when the film

is developed. Just a gilded frame

surrounding a darkness,

limitless and without reason.

Like the wood and steel crutches hanging

from rusted nails in this back room, names

etched along the edges, crutches in every corner

and hanging from the ceiling.

Above the door, one pair intersects

to form a cross, held together

by the belt of a hospital robe.

The pictures of us appear here

years later, taped to this back wall with

hundreds of others, facing our father,

who kneels on an earthen floor by a hole

growing deeper as word

of the healing dirt spreads.

Quixote

Cellophane shimmers
on the nightstand.

A Mexican bar
code just visible: 111-

Moans and spit
amortizing debt,

as in *oh*
and you owe me

nothing but these,
unlike stock,

but rising, wings of
vein, skin.

The dream
of Spain again:

A song at the far
end of a Zurbarán,

binding lamb hoofs
with sweaty hair,

iterating scores of
hidden tendrils

in rivered surrender.
Nectar of bell

filling undocumented
throats of words.

The Only Thing I Imagine Luz Villa Admires about Her Husband's Gun—

is the six-chambered cylinder,

the spinnable heart,

how it clicks into place,

lonely but strong by design.

She understands its negative worth,

how it holds in the dark

and withstands what is held,

how it burns and smells

of smoke when left and left and left.

The Loudspeaker

In the Ogaden desert, they skim it from muddy water,

pour it over cactus meat, ululations crisp as morning birds.

☙

With fossils they tune innards. With tails write.

Pause for good light. Let it pass through remains,

the Loudspeaker warbling in low tones.

☙

In Oaxaca, they carve it of radishes. Contorted

shapes shaved into violins slung into trees,

cutting a thick, rained foliage sonata

for African bees. Some measures drizzling

the branches, others hidden in the roots,

☙

the pulse endlessly trilling

in the City of Angels, where it

resurfaces by the docks:

fifty varieties of night shade and sweet pearl,

fifty sacks of thistle grown entirely by pitch.

෨

As the *what if* of the inflamed song

splits the surface like a whale's tail,

Argentines collected sun-bleached

cardboard in the storm of smells, knowing

hours by the heat of another's body.

෨

Will we hear it en masse,

the solipsistic question: *why do they hate us?* flaking

to an inarticulate texture,

dusty rafters quaking until undone, hornlike,

piece by piece we enter the Loudspeaker

addressed as stranger:

෨

You are the last stranger,

little organ, little ear,

all your lorries loaded with air.

Here we are the spoils:

this breath a wilderness, broken date,

all wound, a wilderness of books becoming wind.

Here we turn like snake tails or great bridal veils

toward the untoward self,

reaching for our own pushing away

as in your voice (long dead)

will reach the shores

of others through calculus, cartoons, used shoes

pausing beneath

public poplars, their golden fans applauding:

Mamá,Mamá,Mama,Mama,Mamá

kissing you, caressing a rhythm.

Empire #4

Mirror

The sun's reflection in a bucket of water just before
a sparrow plunges headfirst, its thirst breaking the light into bits.

Hephaestus knew this was enough. That we wouldn't like
our noses, those bumps along the chin, thin spear of hair calling us

widows, crevasses along the eyes. Why repeat them?
Did he think upon reflection we wouldn't select?

Did he believe we would see smile and frown as round gestures
cradling the invisible—*to feel*—?

The tall mirror inlaid in the hallway never cracked.
You can see it if you visit Versailles.

Polished metal, the echoes in the glaze are ways
to become a stranger again and again.

At the dressing table, one hand in the dim light reaches
as trains rush through tunnels under the city.

One hand and then the other gather hair away from the neck.
I can't see you anymore, we say, *I'm seeing someone else.*

Ode to Water

The squeegee works its way across the glass

in strokes, the blade cuts light from dust

as bird droppings blacken and ink their way down.

I could be two or three the way I'm drawn

to count the sliding drops rushing to swallow

others from behind. I am impressed

with every small performance, the air

as it transforms the light, revealing how

the window warps the telephone pole, my

mother's unconscious, watery arm, raised

to not greet me, four, five, six times. I love

this home where something always shines. Where

a pane reflects everything and you stare

through it. But quickly I'll be asked to come

and join her. "You can at least help me out,"

she mouths as if into a barrel filled

with water. "I will," I think, grabbing rags

and heading through the back doorway. The light

outside is scattering around the trees,

around my shadowy dark circumference.

Portrait of a Voice

Even though
I am   blind,

I catch   each   disturbance
of atmosphere,   engineering
rhythmic   disappearances,
one cloud   canceling   another,

the squall made   more
acute   by   my   lack of skin.

See that man,   *his back   shading*
the boy   *next to him,*
the boy   *standing   rod stiff and ashen,*
his   *amber*   *eyes,*

rent by   *branches   trapped*
inside,   *look*
blankly   *out at*   *me*

who   *can't*   *see,*   *who,*

to get the   presence
of   *absence*

right,   *spent*   *nights*
singing   *to each*
of   *you*
                    at a time

close to   *a burning,*   *promising*

exchange.

Scree

The scholars of war are counting again.
In the dream of the finish line
toward which he steps,

he sips what he's been told,
bracer warming limbs,
while he forgets years

stationed by a tree
fried at the outskirts
of the city.

He dreams a dog, a scent, tortillas
torn by hand, of licking
the crock and waiting for more.

Waiting in the night for the night
hand, the night hip.

Briefly buried by an avalanche
he has no recollection of.
It all makes sense:

the weather report,
tiny salmon in his throat,

the doctors, scholars

of war counting again.

He survives on powdered meat alone

until one night asleep, mouth agape,

he inhales.

Bright orange dust cakes him,

each particle

glinting like a fact.

Note: The phrase, "scholars of war," is taken from Allen Ginsberg's poem "Howl."

Memory from a Bone Sample

Flags in the winter sky,

you at the pillars

with your tongue in a glass box,

ashes settling on carts and props.

Or mammal carcasses hauled on board,

the subcutaneous fat spread around.

I finger a piece of your vestment

in the checkpoint basement.

Sparks in the dark-blue flicker of

book-filled cisterns: summer crops.

Missing Mariachi

Maybe one of the trumpeters, head held back,

haloed by a black felt sombrero, maybe the wax-mustached

guitarist in mid-strum, or the round one with a guitarrón.

Hard to tell; they're so small and so many standing two inches

high on the living room mantel. They appeared one day

like distant relatives you're supposed to love. It was easy

when one wasn't missing. I simply smiled when my mother

purchased dime-size *zarapes,* tiny blue paper flowers, microphone

stands made of bobby-pins, miniature earthenware jugs

and plastic shrubs materializing by a wife and kids off to the side

eating the smallest pink ice cream cones. It was only a matter of time.

Soon they might inhabit bookshelves, window ledges,

computer tops, insinuating songs neighbors haven't heard

before: a *huapango* littered with irrational rhythms

or a *son jarocho,* the harp and the horse bone baptizing us with sweat.

Combustion

I trip trying to retrieve
a bucket from the washroom,
cold tile joining my mother's
voice. My brother,
half asleep, smoke

billowing behind him.
Comic books catch
and curl: *The Story of X,*
The Last Man.

Embers storm the heavy
winter curtain, burning
dime-size holes until
the panel catches
in a triangle of light.

Or maybe flames come
first, melting
shortwave radios of
army men near the Thien Hau Temple,
where miners fashion tin babies
for export, slim as fish scales.

In yet another version, I have
no brother. My mother
and father are wedding under
a canopy stippled with mirrors
in a pattern of flight.

Railroad ties and currency
are used for bonfires.
All is paved
with combustion.

The Wild Pink

I threw it and it flew away.

It grew surly and phosphorus first,

sobbed and wanted to know why.

Demanded breezes and geothermal fuel.

It fooled no one. It drooled.

It sobbed and wanted to know why.

I panicked, asked it, *stay awhile.*

It chose a room and borrowed

a blazer, the one with the copper thread.

It said I drank from impossible bottles at night,

buried letters in bags of grain,

sustained injuries

that made me difficult to understand.

Out of modesty I hid

the knife and turned up the music. It loved

to dance, first with me, then with itself.

After the Death of Pancho Villa

If she's not visiting

his museum

to oil the saddle,

dust his bronze bust—

meticulous

with the auricles of his ears

and the furrows

of his mustache—

she tends

to be outside

with her chickens,

away from the procession

of visitors who want

to inspect the frayed gold

insignia he wore

on his Stetson,

or the five sabers

saluting on the wall,

who want to know if

a small dark spot is blood.

The Last Line

Ask the last one what she is waiting for

on the beveled street behind the white horses

and hypnotists, and she'll say nothing

as she taps the cudgel against her knee.

One of the women, far ahead in gold

earrings and folkloric dress, looks like her sister, but

darker, finer. Is there something beyond

the rise? Silent, she wipes her bleary eyes,

shifts weight to her wet foot tethered

to the morning wind as the turbines begin:

acknowledgments

To the editors of the following journals in which some of these poems (or earlier versions of them) originally appeared:

Afugabe: "Memory from a Bone Sample"
Cortland Review: "Many Years After"
Event Magazine: "After the Death of Pancho Villa"
From the Fishhouse: "After Sex"
Gulf Coast: "Sappho," "Migration"
The Homestead Review: "Cortés and Cannon"
Indiana Review: "The Only Thing I Imagine Luz Villa Admires about Her Husband's Gun—"
Louisiana Literature: "A Question," "A Daughter"
The Massachusetts Review: "Here We Are"
New England Review: "Mexico, 1910"
Ocho #15: "The Wild Pink," "Between the House and the Hill," "Esta Palabra"
Pistola: "Missing Mariachi," " Primavera," "Ode to Water"
The Rumpus: "On Language"
The Seattle Review: "Blue Alert," "The Last Line"
Seneca Review: "Chimayo, New Mexico"
Solo: "Christmas 1964," "Caught in the Eye of the Sun"
2002 Women in Literature and Letters Anthology: Mamibaile: "Empire #1: Five and Dime Store, 1949"

To the following organizations for their material and financial support: the Vermont Studio Center, Hall Farm Center for Arts and Education, the Barbara Deming Memorial Fund, WILL: Women in Literature and Letters, Poetry for the People, Bread Loaf Writers' Conference, and the National Endowment for the Arts;

To Eduardo C. Corral and David Buuck for offering critical feedback;

To Shane Book for all of it including many editorial comments, discussions, book suggestions, support, and inspiration;

To my editor Kristin Buckles, production editor Nancy Arora, and the University of Arizona Press staff for their dedication to the artful rendering of this book;

To my loving family: Luis and Lupe Candelaria, Maria Christina Candelaria, Gabriela Candelaria, Juan Candelaria, Leticia Allen, Maria "Pete" Bagula, and my nephew, nieces, cousins, tíos, and tías for their laughter, wit, and joy;

To Aaron Brick for his knowledge of the Spanish language, curiosity, and love;

To friends and teachers who have guided, inspired, and encouraged me: Philip Levine, Galway Kinnell, Sharon Olds, the P4P poets at UC Berkeley, Brian Spears, Gregory Pardlo, Michael Collier, Samantha Liapes, Stacy Mohammed, Kimberly Jean Smith, Angie Cruz, Marta Lucía Vargas, Camille Dungy, Fran Lozano, Kinan Valdez, Scott Browning, Christopher D. Meyer, Adrienne Torf, James Hall, Erin Crook, Celia Marquez, Ruben Gonzales, Gina Franco, Francisco Aragón, Annabrown Griswold, and Lauren Muller.

about the author

Xochiqueztal Candelaria was raised in San Juan Bautista, California, holds degrees from the University of California–Berkeley and New York University, and is a faculty member at San Francisco City College. Her work has appeared in *The Nation, New England Review, Gulf Coast, Seneca Review,* and other magazines. She has also written articles for the online journal *Solo Ella.* Ms. Candelaria received fellowships from UC Berkeley, New York University, the Vermont Studio Center, Bread Loaf Writers' Conference (2005, 2006), Hall Farm Center for Arts and Education, the National Hispanic Foundation for the Arts, the Barbara Deming Memorial Fund, and the LEF Foundation. She was the winner of the 2006 Dorothy Sargent Rosenberg Poetry Prize, the Louisiana Literature Prize for Poetry, and the Gulf Coast Poetry Prize. In 2009, Ms. Candelaria received an individual literature fellowship from the National Endowment for the Arts.

Library of Congress Cataloging-in-Publication Data

Candelaria, Xochiquetzal, 1973–

  Empire : poems / by Xochiquetzal Candelaria.

    p. cm. — (Camino del sol)

  ISBN 978-0-8165-2882-0 (pbk. : alk. paper)

  I. Title.

  PS3603.A5358E67 2011

  811'.6–dc22

                    2010026533